3 —

The
Quotable
John
Wayne

THE QUOTABLE JOHN WAYNE

The Grit and Wisdom of an American Icon

COMPILED AND EDITED BY CAROL LEA MUELLER

TAYLOR TRADE PUBLISHING
Lanham • New York • Boulder • Toronto • Plymouth, UK

Published by Taylor Trade Publishing
An imprint of The Rowman & Littlefield Publishing Group, Inc.
4501 Forbes Boulevard, Suite 200, Lanham, Maryland 20706

Estover Road, Plymouth PL6 7PY, United Kingdom

Distributed by NATIONAL BOOK NETWORK

Library of Congress Cataloging-in-Publication Data
Wayne, John, 1907-1979.
   The quotable John Wayne : the grit and wisdom of an American
icon / edited by Carol Lea Mueller. — 1st Taylor Trade Publishing ed.
   p. cm.
   ISBN-13: 978-1-58979-332-3 (cloth : alk. paper)
   ISBN-10: 1-58979-332-3 (cloth : alk. paper)
   1. Wayne, John, 1907-1979—Quotations. 2. Quotations, American.
I. Mueller, Carol Lea, 1940- II. Title.

PN2287.W36A25 2007
791.4302'8092—dc22

                                                                2007010445

∞™ The paper used in this publication meets the minimum
requirements of American National Standard for Information
Sciences—Permanence of Paper for Printed Library Materials,
ANSI/NISO Z39.48-1992.

Manufactured in the United States of America.

This book is dedicated to SSG Roland L. Reyes,
Currently on his second tour of duty in Iraq and Afghanistan,
and to his entire HHC 635th Regimental Support Group,
Olathe, Kansas, United States Army
Operation Iraqi Freedom (06–08)
Camp Arifjan, Kuwait—

Just an ordinary soldier, among many, who represents
All his fellow warriors just as John Wayne,
An ordinary actor, has come to represent all America's men
Of valor, always ready to "saddle up" for freedom.

John Wayne was bigger than life. In an age of few heroes, he was the genuine article. But he was more than a hero. He was a symbol of so many of the qualities that made America great. The ruggedness, the tough independence, the sense of personal courage— on and off screen—reflected the best of our national character.
—President Jimmy Carter, 1979

Contents

INTRODUCTION

Tomorrow is the most important thing in life. It comes to us at midnight very clean. It's perfect when it arrives, and it puts itself in our hands and hopes we've learned something from yesterday.
—*John Wayne*

YOU WON'T FIND John Wayne's words in the *Oxford Dictionary of Quotations*, but maybe that's not unfair—he did change the English language for the worse perhaps, with the introduction of such slang phrases as "doing a John Wayne" and "who do you think you are, John Wayne?" His critics always said he was too simple and too blunt, he saw things in black and white, and he was "just another" stubborn conservative full of hot air, like Ronald Reagan: Leave the running of the world to those sophisticated liberals was the idea. And then the Wall fell.

So, you may fairly ask, "Why another book on John Wayne? He's been dead over a quarter of a century. What's left to be said?" Sure, if you do a Google search on "John Wayne," you are presented with a couple of million items relating to the Duke. The answer is that this book speaks in Wayne's own voice and that, for the first time, his words are put together in a readable, memorable format that reveals, along with his grit, a quick and wicked sense of humor. It also becomes clear that the only roles he chose were those that had lines consistent with his beliefs; he never wanted to be ashamed of what he did or said on or off the screen.

He always resisted the pleas to write an autobiography, responding that "Those who like me already know me, and those who don't like me wouldn't want to read about me anyway." He was wrong, of course. We are all, liberal and conservative alike, still fascinated by his reel- and real-life personas, and yet so few members of our current generation realize the effect that the power of his personal example along with his words and ideas has had upon our image as a nation.

What makes his character and words inspire us, despite their personal flaws, and still have resonance with us is that in his on-screen presentation and demeanor, he always tried to exemplify American ideals in the best sense of the word. We want to listen to this man, this totally honest, credible American even when we disagree, even when he's not acting, because we believe in him as an American—as an Icon with a capital *I* along with Mom and Apple Pie.

Amazingly, the cowboy ideal he personified is also alive and thriving in a new millennium: Basic tenets such as being true to your word and the understanding that character really does matter are still being championed as American ideals. That rugged independence and stoic nature of the legendary "outsider" cowboy is still being portrayed on the screen; we see the continuing struggle of men striving to be true to themselves and redeeming themselves when they do fail.

One cannot help but wonder in the aftermath of the tragedy of September 11, 2001, if Wayne's many heroic roles influenced our leaders on that horrific day and gave them the necessary strength. John Wayne wasn't there to lead or console us. Or was he? He certainly had shown us how to be Americans, how heroes behaved, and how to handle adversity. New York Mayor Rudy Giuliani *was* John Wayne, perhaps, on that day, as was our President George W. Bush and all the firefighters, police officers, Flight 93 passengers, and other countless heroes who will inspire future generations.

For once, I like to think, John Wayne, the Duke, was watching the action and was proud to be an American all over again.

Carol Lea Mueller

Santa Cruz, California

July 2006

God and Country

There is no one who more exemplifies the devotion to
our country, its goodness, its industry, and
its strength than John Wayne.
—President Ronald Reagan

John Wayne is loved the world over as a man who
represents independence, the love of freedom, and the
hearty strength of character which made our country
great. For audiences at home, John Wayne, through his
films, remains an authentic folk hero. In this era of
shifting moral values and cynicism, he has made a
contribution of inestimable value to American culture
and is deserving of this tribute [a Congressional Gold
Medal] from the American people.
—Gregory Peck

No man's lifetime of work has better expressed the land
of the free and the home of the brave. No man's lifetime
of work has given proof to the world that our flag is
still there. John Wayne is in truth a star-spangled man
who so proudly we hail.
—Frank Sinatra

THERE WAS NEVER any doubt that John Wayne was a patriot. He expressed that spirit in words and in his life and in the roles he chose to play; he was also a man of faith. The following are all off-screen quotations from the Duke:

"Sure, I wave the American flag. Do you know a better one?"

"We've made mistakes along the way, but that's no reason to start tearing up the best flag God ever gave to any country."

"I am an old-fashioned, honest-to-goodness, flag-waving patriot."

"It's kind of a sad thing when a normal love of country makes you a 'super patriot.'"

"Give the American people a good cause and there's nothing they can't lick."

"I think government is a necessary evil, like say, motion picture agents."

"If everything isn't black and white, I say, 'Why the hell not?'"

"Screw ambiguity. Perversion and corruption masquerade as ambiguity. I don't like ambiguity. I don't trust ambiguity."

"America is the land of freedom and that's the way I enjoy living."

"Our country thrives on change . . . no guns or bombs or Army coups . . . just the biggest and best weapon of all, our right to vote. X's on paper. The ballot box, a good thing."

"You've got the strongest hand in the world. That's right. Your hand. The hand that marks the ballot. The hand that pulls the voting lever. Use it, will you."

"Very few of the so-called liberals are open-minded
... they shout you down and won't let you speak if you
disagree with them."

"Sure, I love my country with all her faults. I'm not
ashamed of that, never have been and never will be. I
was proud when President Nixon ordered the mining
of Haiphong Harbor, which we should have done long
before, because I think we were helping a brave little
country defend herself against Communist invasion.
That's what I tried to show in *The Green Berets* and I
took plenty of abuse from the critics."

On American spirit: "It's an outlook, an attitude."

"When I was a sophomore at USC [University of
Southern California], I was a socialist, pretty much to
the left but not when I left the university. I quickly got
wise. I'd read about what had happened to Russia in
1917 when the Communists took over—Communism
just doesn't work."

"I never felt I needed to apologize for my patriotism. I felt that if there were Communists in the business—and I knew there were—then they ought to go over to Russia and try enjoying freedom there."

"If you're in a fight, you must fight to win, and in those early years of the Cold War, I strongly believed that our country's fundamental values were in jeopardy. I think that the Communists proved my point over the years."

Of his politics ruining his career, Wayne said, "I was thirty-second in the box office polls when I accepted the presidency of the Motion Picture Alliance for the Preservation of American Ideals. When I left office eight years later, somehow the folks who buy tickets had made me number one."

"Socialism isn't going to stop the selfishness of human behavior. It isn't going to stop the greed. If you take twenty dollars and give a dollar to every sonuvabitch in a room and come back a year later, one of the bastards will have most of the money. It's just human nature and you're not going to whip it with a lot of laws."

On the plights of the Native American: "I'm quite sure that the concept of a government-run reservation would have an ill effect on anyone. But that seems to be what the socialists are working for now—to have everyone cared for from cradle to grave."

"Mine is a rebellion against the monotony of life. The rebellion in these kids, particularly the SDS'ers and those groups, seems to be a kind of dissension by rote."

On the negative influence of liberal ideology on America's youth: "They work against the natural loyalties and ideals of our kids, filling them with fear and doubt and hate and downgrading patriotism and all our heroes of the past."

In 1960: "These are perilous times. The eyes of the world are on us. We must sell America to countries threatened with Communist domination."

When asked at the 1969 Republican Convention about his political ambitions, the Duke answered, "I'm about as political as a Bengal tiger."

"Success is not measured by your wealth, but in your worth. . . . Honorable men and women have a right to stand up for the things they hold dear. . . . It's the American way."

"I have found a certain type calls himself a liberal. . . . Now I always thought I was a liberal. I came up terribly surprised one time when I found out that I was a 'Right-Wing Conservative Extremist' when *I* listened to everybody's point of view that I ever met, and *then* I decided how I should feel. But this so-called Liberal group, Jesus, they never listen to your point of view."

"I was invited at first to a couple of Communist cell meetings, and I played the lamb to listen to 'em for a while, but it was just a bunch of commie b.s."

In 1948 as a member of the Motion Picture Alliance for the Preservation of American Ideals, Wayne was alarmed at the growth and influence of Communism in Hollywood: "Actually we were the real liberals. We believed in freedom. We believed in the individual and his rights. We hated Soviet Communism because it was against all religion, because it trampled on the individual, because it was a slave society."

On America's freedom: "People can live free, talk free, go and come, buy or sell, be drunk or sober, however they choose."

"Listen, I spoke to the Man up there on many occasions; I've always had deep faith that there is a Supreme Being, there has to be. To me that's just a normal thing to have that kind of faith. The fact that He's let me stick around a little longer, or She's let me stick around a little longer, certainly goes great with me—and I want to hang around as long as I'm healthy and not in anybody's way."

"A man's got to have a code, a creed to live by, no matter his job."

"When the road looks rough ahead, remember the Man upstairs and the word *Hope*. Hang on to both and tough it out."

About dropping out of the University of Southern California while planning to be an attorney, Wayne said, "If it hadn't been for football and the fact that my leg broke [with the loss of an athletic scholarship] and I had to go into the movies to eat, why who knows, I might have turned out to be a liberal Democrat."

In the fall of 1968, Governor George Wallace, who was running on the American Party ticket, asked the Duke to be his vice-presidential running mate. His was a polite, succinct response: "Sorry, I'm a Nixon man."

On liberals and the Vietnam War: "Once you go over there, you won't be middle of the road. Bobby Kennedy and Arkansas Senator Fulbright and all those [expletive] let's-be-sweet-to-our-dear-enemy's guys, all they're doing is helping the Reds and hurting their own country."

In 1977, invited to pre-inaugural events by President-Elect Jimmy Carter, Wayne spoke at a Kennedy Center celebration: "I'm privileged to be present and accounted for in this Capitol of freedom, to watch a common man take on uncommon responsibilities that he has won fair and square by stating his case to the American people—not by bloodshed, beheadings, and riots at the palace gates. I'm considered a member of the opposition, the loyal opposition. Accent on the *loyal*. I'd have it no other way."

"My hope and prayer is that everyone know and love our country for what she really is and what she stands for."

On some American politicians: "They're not willing to take the responsibility of leadership instead of check-ing polls and listening to the few that scream."

"Watergate is a sad and tragic incident in our history. . . . Men abused power, but the system still works. . . . Men lied and perjured themselves but the system still works."

Against a 1972 California referendum for government censorship of films, Wayne said in radio commercials, "You don't get rid of a bad situation with a badly written law . . . or cut off a foot to cure a sore toe."

After the armed Duke had chased a burglar out of his home, he had this to say to those who supported gun control: "I'm sorry they feel that way but ya know, the first time they come across some bastard breakin' into their home or tryin' to take one of their kids, they'd be damn glad to have a gun around."

"This new thing of genuflecting to the downtrodden, I don't go along with that. We ought to go back to praising the kids who get good grades, instead of making excuses for the ones who shoot the neighborhood groceryman."

He was against "these people who carry placards to save the life of some criminal, yet have no thought for the innocent victim."

He had a stock response to hate mail in regard to his politics: "You may disagree completely with what I say, but I will defend to the death my right to say it."

It has been claimed that the Duke was in a Las Vegas nightclub one night, and the performers asked him what his favorite song was so they could play it. His response was, "No, if you play my favorite song, everyone will have to stand up."

"I think that the loud roar of irresponsible liberalism . . . is being quieted down by a reasoning public. I think the pendulum is swinging back. We're remembering that the past can't be so bad. We built a nation on it. We have to look to tomorrow."

FAMILY AND FRIENDSHIP

*I have never been in trouble or needed help at any time
in my life that I didn't first pick up the phone and call
Duke, and within five minutes, I had what I wanted or
what I requested, or what I needed. And he never asked
for a thank you. He wouldn't think of that. . . . He has
a very soft heart and if you do make a mistake, he will
bend those rules he lives by, not for himself, but to
forgive you. And that is friendship and love.*
—Maureen O'Hara

*I met Duke in 1952 when we made a movie together,
and it was Duke who suggested me for Matt Dillon in
the television series* Gunsmoke. *He was a real friend.
He was honest, strong, independent, and proud. He's
exactly the kind of man he portrayed in* The Shootist.
*We didn't know it then, but John Wayne was telling us
the rules he lived by, on screen and off.*
—James Arness

*Being the son of John Wayne has just been the greatest.
I couldn't imagine being the son of anybody else. He
was a great dad and a great friend and gave me
incredible opportunities.*
—Patrick Wayne

I didn't know until recently the kinds of things they have been saying about my dad in the papers and magazines. The ones that don't know him sure irritate me. He doesn't talk or act brash like they say. You should see how gentle he is when he wakes up my little sister and me.

—*Ethan Wayne*

Now, in his own words, here is John Wayne on family and friendship:

"I am a demonstrative man, a baby picker-upper, a hugger, and a kisser—that's my nature."

"Any man who would make an X-rated movie ought to have to take his daughter to see it."

"I've always followed my father's advice: He told me, first, to always keep my word and, second, to never insult anybody unintentionally. If I insult you, you can be damn sure I intend to. And, third, he told me not to go around looking for trouble."

In the summer of 1918, Duke's paper route helped pay the family bills: "Times were hard then. I didn't mind if my folks needed some of my money. Dad would have given me the shirt off his back."

"The biggest trial of my young life was shepherding my little brother around. Wherever I went, Bob had to follow."

"I became a confirmed reader when I was growing up in Glendale and could read before going to school. . . . I've loved reading all my life."

On the naming of his first son Michael: "Well, I sure as hell wasn't going to name my firstborn Marion [Wayne's own given first name]—any kid called Marion's gonna have a rough ride and I should know."

"I've had three wives, six children, and six grandchildren, and I still don't understand women."

On Wayne's marriage to his second wife, Chata: "Our marriage was like shaking two volatile chemicals in [a] jar."

"I drink for comradeship, and when I drink for comradeship, I don't bother to keep count."

On Wayne's third wife, Pilar: "I can tell you why I love her. I have a lust for her dignity. I look at her wonderfully classic face, and I see hidden in it a sense of humor that I love. I think of wonderful, exciting, decent things when I look at her."

Of Pilar's request that the word *obey* be dropped from their wedding vows, Wayne agreed, saying, "None of the others ever obeyed me anyway!"

Wayne spent the Christmas of 1954 with his new wife, Pilar, and his four children by his first wife and said, "This is what it's all about, what I've always wanted—a successful career, a wife I love who loves me back, my family around."

"You know, I hear everybody talking about the generation gap. Frankly, sometimes I don't know what they're talking about. Heck, by now I should know a little about it, if ever I'm going to. I have seven kids and eighteen grandkids and I don't seem to have any trouble talking to any of them. Never had, and don't intend to start now."

His daughter Aissa tells about the time her father found out that she and several friends had been caught smoking marijuana in a neighbor's home. He said to her, "We need to talk." Sitting with her at the kitchen table he calmly said, "Aissa, I love you very much. The people that gave you that stuff, they don't love you the way that I do. You can take their word that this stuff is good, or you can listen to me when I tell you it's bad." She says that that had more of an effect than rage or self-righteousness would have.

Duke said of Margot Fonteyn, the internationally famous ballerina who had married his Panamanian friend Roberto Arias, "She was the most beautiful person I've known in my whole life." (When an assassination attempt on her husband in 1965 left him a paraplegic, Fonteyn was completely devoted to him until his death in 1989.)

"I have tried to live my life so that my family would love me and my friends respect me. The others can do whatever the hell they please."

"God, how I hate solemn funerals. When I die, take me into a room and burn me. Then my family and a few good friends should get together, have a few good belts and talk about the crazy old times we all had together."

No matter who he was introduced to, he responded, "Just call me Duke."

When asked if football helped in life, Wayne said, "Do you know a better way to learn respect from someone than to have him across the line of scrimmage from you? Do you think the color of your skin or the amount of your father's property or your social position helps you there?"

Wayne gave this advice to his daughter Aissa: "Never think anyone is better than you, but never assume you're superior to anyone else. Try and be decent to everyone, until they give you reason not to."

On his friend Maureen O'Hara: "Maureen is not like most other women. She didn't mind you using four-letter words around her, which I tend to do—often—and she didn't get all girly and dainty, and yet she is still totally feminine. She's like a guy almost. . . . She is a woman who speaks her mind and that impressed me, despite my old-fashioned chauvinistic ways! She is feminine and beautiful, but there's something about her that makes her more like a man . . . it's her stubbornness and her willingness to stand up to anyone."

When Aissa was a little girl, he told her, "If anything happens to me, just look up and find a big star in the sky. That'll be me. I'll always be there watching over you."

After recovering successfully from his bout with lung cancer, Wayne said in a public service message for the

National Cancer Society, "Get a checkup. Talk to someone you like into getting a checkup. Nag someone you love into getting a checkup. And while you're at it, send a check to the American Cancer Society. It's great to be alive."

"I licked the Big C. I know the Man upstairs will pull the plug when he wants to, but I don't want to end my life being sick. I want to go out on two feet, in action." (He went public about his cancer despite warnings that it would hurt his image.)

As a daughter from his first marriage was planning her wedding, Wayne found out his third wife, Pilar, was pregnant with their first child and told her, "This is my second chance at being a father. It isn't often a man gets a second chance in life. This time, I swear I'll do it right."

Giving the eulogy at his lifelong friend's funeral, he said of Ward Bond, "We were the closest of friends, from school days right on through. This is the way Ward would have wanted it—to look out on the faces of good friends. He was a wonderful, generous, big-hearted man."

When asked if he believed in God, he replied, "There must be some higher power or how else does all this work?"

Wayne was a Mason and, when younger, had joined the DeMolay youth group and said of his experience, "I was overwhelmed by the feeling of friendship, comradeship, and brotherhood. . . . DeMolay will always hold a deep spot in my heart."

Wayne always watched out for his family. When he was offered $1 million to appear in a Gillette ad on a merchant ship with a young lieutenant, he was told that an unknown would play the lieutenant at minimum wage. Duke told them, "I'll tell you what! I'll do it on one condition. You give the million dollars to my son, Pat, to act the lieutenant and give me the scale instead."

Wayne was devastated when his lifelong pal Ward Bond died suddenly of a heart attack at the age of fifty-five.

Wayne's friend Loretta Young tried to console him by telling him to try praying. The next time she saw him, she asked how he was doing, and he said, "I took your advice. Somebody upstairs listened. It kind of lightened the load."

THE OLD WEST

*Herman Melville said the American Adam is like the
original Adam. He comes out of the earth at God's call.
He's not brought from any previous descendants. Well,
that was what the idea was of America. Here we had
this great continent. It was a clean slate, a fresh start.
We were not going to be like any other country, and so
this Adam, who is naïve in some ways, not learned in
the ways of the world, has an earthy wisdom from
contact with the great outdoors, and, you know, Wayne
just breathes that, moves that, walks that.*
　—Garry Wills

*No film actor had greater integrity or stature. He
represented the American folk hero at his best.*
　—Hal Wallis

*Young man, you represent the cavalry officer more than
any man in uniform.*
　—General Douglas MacArthur

*Wayne has never underestimated one of the greatest
axioms of a good Western—a good silent man with a
horse is better than two hours of talk.*
　—David Sutton

*How can I hate John Wayne upholding Goldwater and
yet love him tenderly when he abruptly takes Natalie
Wood into his arms in the last reel of* The Searchers?
. . . I was moved to tears in a darkened theatre in Paris.
—Jean-Luc Godard

THE DUKE'S LOVE of the Western movie genre
and respect for the characters he played was
boundless; he willingly defended them and their ideals.
Westerns were opportunities to convey an important
aspect of American history, part of this country's heritage, to a wide audience. He boldly protected the
cowboy and gunfighter and expressed resentment of
any manipulation of what he saw as simple basic tra-
ditional values and truths. Here, in his own words, is
the American West:

"Every country in the world loved the folklore of the
West—the music, the dress, the excitement, everything
that was associated with the opening of a new territory.
It took everybody out of their own little world. The
cowboy lasted a hundred years, created more songs and
prose and poetry than any other folk figure. The closest thing was the Japanese samurai. Now, I wonder
who'll continue it?"

"The West—the very words go straight to that place of the heart where Americans feel the spirit of pride in their Western heritage—the triumph of personal courage over any obstacle, whether nature or man."

"Westerns are closer to art than anything else in the motion picture business."

"Courage is being scared to death—and saddling up anyway."

Of acting in a Western portraying the struggle of American settlers threatened by the British and the Indians in the wild frontier, Wayne said, "I played one cautious part in my life, in *Allegheny Uprising*."

"Put a man on a horse, and right off you've got the making of something magnificent. Physical strength, speed where you can feel it, plus heroism. And the hero, he's big and strong. You pit another strong man against him, with both their lives at stake, and right there's a simplicity of conflict you just can't beat."

"Nobody should see this movie [*The Alamo*] unless he believes in heroes."

"Don't even for a minute make the mistake of looking down your nose at Westerns. They're art—the good ones, I mean. Sure, they're simple, but simplicity is art. They deal in life and sudden death and primitive struggle, and with the basic emotions—love, hate, and anger—thrown in. We'll have Western films as long as the cameras keep turning. The fascination that the Old West has will never die."

After recommending James Arness for his television role in the beloved series *Gunsmoke*, Wayne introduced the first episode in 1955 with these words: "Good evening. My name is John Wayne. Some of you have seen me before. I hope so—I've been kickin' around Hollywood for a long time. I've made a lot of pictures out here, all kinds. Some of them are Westerns, and that's what I'm here to tell you about tonight—a Western. A new television show called *Gunsmoke*. I knew there was only one man to play it—James Arness. He's a young fella and may be new to some of you. But I've worked with him, and I predict he'll be a big star. And now I'm proud to present *Gunsmoke*."

Both Wayne and director Howard Hawks and a few others stood apart in their critical view of the successful *High Noon* because they both felt it was not true to the West or the America they believed in. Most historians agree that most town folk stood by their lawmen in times of trouble. In an interview, Wayne explained his thoughts: "Everyone says *High Noon* was a great picture because Tiomkin wrote some great music for it and because Gary Cooper and Grace Kelly were in it. In the picture, four guys come into town to gun down the sheriff. He goes to church and asks for help and the guys go, 'Oh well, oh gee.' And the women stand up and say, 'You rats, you rats.' So Cooper goes out alone. It's the most un-American thing I ever saw in my whole life. The last thing in the picture is ole Coop throwing a United States marshal's badge in the dirt." Hawks agreed that Cooper being saved by his Quaker wife was utter nonsense, and the pair teamed up to show how it should have been done in *Rio Bravo*.

"Television has a tendency to reach a little—in their Westerns, they are getting away from the simplicity and the fact that those men were fighting the elements and the rawness of nature and didn't have time for the 'couch work.'"

When asked how he would play Genghis Khan, the Duke replied, "I see him as a gunfighter."

On his making of *The Alamo*: "I'd read up on the history of our country, and I'd become fascinated with the story of the Alamo. To me it represents the fight for freedom, not just in America, but in all countries. . . . I hope that seeing the battle of the Alamo will remind Americans that liberty and freedom don't come cheap. I hope our children will get a sense of our glorious past and appreciate the struggle our ancestors made for the precious freedom we now enjoy—and sometimes take for granted."

About the story of the Alamo, Wayne also said, "It had to be made into a motion picture. It has the raw and tender stuff of immortality, peopled by hard-living, hard-loving men whose women matched them in creating a pattern of freedom and liberty."

A few years after the original release, Wayne had this to say: "I wish they would re-release *The Alamo* today. There's more to that movie than my damn conservative attitude."

WIT WITH THE GRIT

He was a big, big chunk of America. Wayne meant a lot to America. He loved to promote America. He stood for America. I don't think he saw himself as a symbol. He just wanted to do the things he wanted to do, and those things were right for America.
—Bob Hope

MORE THAN ANY other actor, John Wayne was willing to let the joke be on him—he accepted the many parodies of himself with mild amusement and was a willing participant in many sketches on television—once mocking his tough guy image by appearing in a huge bunny suit! So, these following words are typical of his sense of humor:

When asked how he wanted to be remembered, the Duke replied, "Feo, Fuerte y Formal" from a Spanish proverb. (He was ugly, strong, and had dignity).

"I'm an American actor. I work with my clothes on. I have to. Riding a horse can be pretty tough on your legs and elsewhere."

"Damn, I'm the stuff men are made of!"

About running for public office: "I can't afford the cut in pay; besides, who in the world would vote for an actor?"

When he was rudely challenged by Harvard Lampoon to visit them for the Hasty Pudding Award, Wayne wrote back, "Sorry to note that there is a weakness in your breeding, but there is a ray of hope in the fact that you are conscious of it." (He did go and arrived in a borrowed tank.)

When facing the Harvard Lampoon audience that hoped to embarrass him, he was asked about his phony hairpiece. The Duke quickly responded, "It's not phony. It's real hair. Of course, it's not mine, but it's real."

Wayne was also asked at Harvard if President Nixon had ever given him any suggestions for his movies. He replied, "No. They've all been successful."

"Nixon needs more training as an actor."

Another impudent Harvard questioner asked, "Is it true that since you've lost weight, your horse's hernia has cleared up?" The immediate response from Wayne was, "No, he died and we canned him, which is what you are eating at the Harvard Club."

A student reporter from Harvard asked sarcastically if he looked at himself as an "American Legend." Wayne replied, "Well, not being a *Harvard* man, I don't look at myself any more than necessary."

Responding to this final, ridiculous question: "Why do you refuse to allow midgets in your major films?" He shot back with, "It's too hard to find their mouths to punch."

Asked if being hounded for autographs upsets him, Wayne responded, "No, it will upset me when they stop asking!"

"A man's character and personality is made up by the incidents in his life. Mine has been made up of one thing in *reel* life, and possibly every dramatic experience that a human being could have in *real* life. Somewhere in between lies John Wayne. I seldom lie."

While shooting *Rio Lobo*, somebody asked Wayne where his dressing room was: "See that nail on the wall?"

"A horse is a horse; it doesn't make a difference what color it is."

While on location in Africa making *Hatari!* he was playing cards one night with fellow actor Red Buttons. Buttons saw a leopard walking out of the bush and quietly told Duke, "There's a leopard walking toward us." Duke replied, "Buttons, see what he wants."

In his acceptance speech for the Academy Award for Best Actor for *True Grit*, Wayne said, "If I'd known this was all it would take, I'd have put that eye patch on forty years ago."

In a teasing note to Gene Autry: "Our trails have crossed and crisscrossed many a time in our careers, both professionally and social. I guess you realize that if I could have picked up a guitar, you'd probably still be in Sapulpa, Oklahoma, tapping that telegraph key, and those California Angels [Autry was their owner] might be the Anaheim Dukes."

In April 1979, he was dying of cancer, but he came to present the Academy Award for Best Picture. Weak and thin, he cautioned his makeup man to use only light powder: "I'd rather not look as if I'd been embalmed just yet." (He was dead three weeks later.)

When presented with his Best Actor Academy Award by Barbra Streisand for *True Grit*, he leaned over, embraced her, and whispered in her ear, "Beginner's luck."

Replying to a reporter's question, "What do you think of women's lib?" he responded, a little tongue-in-cheek, "I think women's lib is fine, as long as they're home by six to cook my dinner."

Spending Christmas aboard his yacht the *Wild Goose*, moored near Mazatlán in Mexico, in lieu of a tree he had the ship decorated with lights. Seeing the spectacular display that evening, he was delighted: "She's lit up more than the old Duke!"

Leaving Massachusetts General Hospital after having a mitral heart valve replaced, he told the staff, "I can't begin to tell you how grateful I am to all of you, but I think you'll understand if I don't suggest we do it all over again sometime."

He made a few appearances on television, choosing mostly comedy bits. In 1962, he had a cameo role in an episode of *The Beverly Hillbillies*. When approached on the issue of payment, he responded, "Give me a fifth of bourbon and that'll square it."

One role he regretted was that of Genghis Khan in *The Conqueror* (1956); he once said that the moral of the movie was "not to make an ass of yourself trying to play parts you're not suited for."

"When people say a John Wayne picture got bad reviews, I always wonder if they know it's a redundant sentence, [but] hell, I don't care. People like my pictures and that's all that counts."

In 1968 on Rowan and Martin's show *Laugh-In*, he chose to read a poem, "The Sky": "The sky is blue, the grass is green. Get off your ass and join the Marines."

"I stick to simple themes. Love. Hate. No nuances. I stay away from psychoanalysts' couch scenes. Couches are good for one thing."

Asked whether Native Americans should be allowed to camp on Alcatraz Island, which they were claiming as their land, Wayne responded, "Well, I don't know of anybody else who wants it. The fellas who were taken off it sure don't want to go back there, including the guards. So far as I am concerned, I think we ought to make a deal with the Indians. They should pay as much for Alcatraz as we paid them for Manhattan. I hope they haven't been careless with their wampum."

"I never trust a man that doesn't drink."

At a television tribute to himself, Wayne delivered a special message to his fans: "And to all you folks out there, I want to thank you for the last fifty years of my career. And I hope I can keep at it another fifty years— or at least until I can get it right!"

His gruff opinion on awards: "You can't eat awards. Nor, more to the point, drink 'em."

On Acting

*As an actor he has an extraordinary gift. A unique
naturalness. A very subtle capacity to think and express
and caress the camera—the audience. A secret between
them. Wayne was a very, very good actor, in the most
highbrow sense of the word.*
—Katharine Hepburn

*He's not something out of a book, governed by acting
rules. He portrays John Wayne, a rugged American guy.
He's not one of those method actors, like they send out
here from drama schools in New York. He's real,
perfectly natural.*
—John Ford

*Good acting exists when an actor thinks and reacts as
much to imaginary situations as those in real life.
Cooper, Wayne, Tracy try not to act but to be
themselves, to respond or react. They refuse to do or
say anything they feel not to be consistent with
their own characters.*
—Lee Strasberg, Actors Studio

HE ALWAYS MADE it look so easy, maybe too easy—but he knew what he was doing.

"I don't act . . . I react."

"The difference between acting and reacting is that in a bad picture, you see them acting all over the place. In a good picture, they react in a logical way to a situation they're in, so the audience can identify with the actors."

"I merely try to act naturally. If I start acting phony on the screen, you start looking at me instead of feeling with me."

"All I do is sell sincerity, and I've been selling the hell out of that ever since I got started."

"I read dramatic lines undramatically and react to situations normally. This is not as simple as it sounds. I've spent a major portion of my life trying to learn to do it well, and I am not past learning yet."

On acting tricks, Wayne said he had two: "One was to stop in the middle of the sentence, so they'll keep looking at me, the other was not to stop at the end, so they don't look away."

"One look that works is better than twenty lines of dialogue. . . . Let those actors who picked their noses get all the dialogue, just give me the close-up of reaction."

"I guess watching famous movie stars gave me some inspiration to try acting. I was a member of the school dramatic society in high school; in a Shakespeare contest in 1925, I delivered Cardinal Wolsey's speech from *Henry VIII*."

Of his acting in early Westerns: "My main duty was to ride, fight, keep my hat on, and at the end of shooting still have enough strength to kiss the girl and ride off on my horse or kiss my horse and ride off on the girl."

"I understand my fans because *I* had idols. They were Harry Carey and Tom Mix."

Of the B-Westerns he made, he said, "Those films offered me regular work and an opportunity to learn my craft."

"I've played the kinda man I'd like to have been."

"I have certain feelings about what I do. I like to play a character that a large number of people can identify with. Whether it's that they can say he's their father, uncle, brother, or whatever. It's human dignity . . . nothing mean or petty, cruel or rough. Tough, that's all right."

"I don't want ever to appear in a film that would embarrass a viewer. A man can take his wife, mother, and daughter to one of my movies and never be ashamed or embarrassed for going."

"I play John Wayne in every part regardless of the character, and I've been doing okay, haven't I?"

His acting advice to fellow actor Michael Caine: "Talk low, talk slow, and don't say too much."

After *Donavan's Reef*, Wayne said, "I never want to play silly old men chasing young girls."

"I wanted to direct from the first time I set foot in a studio, but I was sidetracked by acting for something like thirty years."

"Nobody liked my acting but the public."

"Perhaps other actors can walk away from people and not be friendly and gracious, I cannot." (Wayne was a willing autograph signer.)

"When I started, I knew I was no actor and I went to work on the Wayne thing. It was as deliberate a projection as you'll ever see. I figured I needed a gimmick, so I dreamed up the drawl, the squint, and a way of moving meant to suggest that I wasn't looking for trouble but would just as soon throw a bottle at your head as not."

"When people you work with do their job to make things right and still have time to smile and get along with others, I want them around."

On turning down the role of Harry Callahan in *Dirty Harry*, Wayne wryly said, "How did I ever let that one slip through my fingers?"

"I want to play a real man in all my films, and I define manhood simply: men should be tough, fair, and courageous; never petty, never looking for a fight, but never backing down from one either."

Maurice Zolotow asked Wayne what had set him apart from other cowboy idols. Wayne continued smoking his cigarette a bit and then extinguished it and replied, "John Ford."

On the critics of *The Alamo*: "That little clique back there in the East has taken great personal satisfaction reviewing my politics instead of my pictures, but one day, those doctrinaire liberals will wake up to find the pendulum has swung the other way."

"I won't play anybody dishonest or cruel or mean for no reason. I've killed men on the screen, but it was always because they didn't follow the code."

On the effect of television: "It's hard to get audiences away from other forms of recreation. A few of the older favorites like myself may have given them pleasure in a movie, so some people are more willing to go out of the house to see us."

About the financial ups and downs of his acting career: "Money never made an unhappy person happy, and I'll be damned if losing money is going to make me miserable. Hell, it's just money. I can make more."

MEMORABLE QUOTES
FROM MOVIES

Get back, pilgrim. Legendary movie cowboy John
Wayne has out-shot Clint Eastwood's Dirty Harry,
and has cruised by Tom Cruise. The late actor has been
named as the "Top Money-Maker of All Time" in the
Quigley Publishing Company annual star poll. . . . In
order to compare The Duke's box office sales to that
earned by contemporary stars, a weighted score was
given to the star's ranking for each year.
—San Jose Mercury News, *2005*

JOHN WAYNE, the actor, spoke the following words in his films; John Wayne, the man, stood by them:

"Well, there are some things a man just can't run away from."

—Ringo Kid, *Stagecoach*

"Well, I guess you can't break out of prison and into society in the same week."

—Ringo Kid, *Stagecoach*

In response to Miss Mary, who tells him he's made of granite: "No, Mary, just common clay. It bakes kind of hard in Texas."

—Bob "Shortcut" Seton, *Dark Command*

"And speaking of politics, where we're going there are only two parties: the quick and the dead."

—John Devlin, *Dakota*

"Winning isn't everything, it's the only thing."

—Steve Williams, *Trouble Along the Way*

"We brought nothing into this world, and it's certain we can carry nothing out."

—Thomas Dunson, *Red River*

"Well, if you saw them, sir, they weren't Apaches."

—Capt. York, *Fort Apache*

"Sorry don't get 'er done."

—John T. Chance, *Rio Bravo*

"Life is tough. It's tougher when you're stupid."

—Sgt. John M. Stryker, *Sands of Iwo Jima*

"Line 'em up and head 'em north, Pilgrim."

—Thomas Dunson, *Red River*

"Every time you turn around, expect to see me. 'Cause one time you'll turn around and I'll be there, and I'll kill you."

—Thomas Dunson, *Red River*

"But put out of your mind any romantic ideas that it's a way of glory. It's a life of suffering and hardship, an uncompromising devotion to your oath and your duty."

—Lt. Col. Kirby Yorke, *Rio Grande*

"George, a wonderful thing about Alaska is that matrimony hasn't hit up here yet. Let's keep it a free country!"

—Sam McCord, *North to Alaska*

"Women. Peculiar."

—Sam McCord, *North to Alaska*

"I'm on your side, lady. It's my only politics . . . anti-wife. Any woman who devotes herself to making one man miserable instead of a lot of men happy, don't get my vote."

—Sam McCord, *North to Alaska*

"Out here, due process is a bullet."

—Col. Mike Kirby, *The Green Berets*

"Well, I don't favor talking to vermin, but I'll talk to you just this once. . . . If one of your men cross my land or even touch one of my cows, or do anything to that store, I'm not going to the sheriff, the governor, or the president of the United States. I'm coming to see you."

—John Simpson Chisum, *Chisum*

"I'm looking at a tin star with a drunk pinned on it."

—Cole Thornton, *El Dorado*

"If you can't respect your elders, then I'll just have to teach you to respect your betters."

—Jacob McCandles, *Big Jake*

"All battles are fought by scared men who'd rather be someplace else."

—Capt. Rockwell Torrey, *In Harm's Way*

"This kind of war, you've got to believe in what you're fighting for."

—Col. Joseph Madden, *Back to Bataan*

"Out here a man settles his own problems."

—Tom Doniphon,
The Man Who Shot Liberty Valance

"'Cause even grown men need understanding."

—J. D. Cahill, *Cahill, U.S. Marshal*

"There are a lot of wonderful things written into our Constitution that were meant for honest, decent citizens. I resent the fact that it can be used and abused by the very people who want to destroy it."

—Jim McLain, *Big Jim McLain*

"Republic, I like the sound of the word. Some words give you a feeling. Republic is one of those words that makes me tight in the throat, same tightness a man gets when his baby takes his first step, or his baby shaves, makes his first sound as a man. Some words can give you a feeling that makes your heart warm . . . Republic is one of those words."

—Col. Davy Crockett, *The Alamo*

"A lot of guys make mistakes, I guess, but every one we make, a whole stack of chips goes with it. We make a mistake, and some guy don't walk away—forevermore he don't walk away."

—Sgt. John M. Stryker, *Sands of Iwo Jima*

"Yup. The end of a way of life. Too bad. It's a good way. Wagons forward! Yo!"

—Hondo Lane, *Hondo*

"I've got a saddle older than you." (Line addressed to Ann-Margret, who lets him know she is available.)

—Lane, *The Train Robbers*

"There's right and there's wrong. You gotta do one or the other. You do the one and you're living. You do the other and you may be walking around, but in reality you're dead as a beaver hat."

—Col. Davy Crockett, *The Alamo*

"It was like I was empty. Well, I'm not empty anymore. That's what's important, to feel useful in this old world, to hit a lick against what's wrong for what's right even though you get walloped."

—Col. Davy Crockett, *The Alamo*

"No woman is going to get me hog-tied and branded!"

—Rocklin, *Tall in the Saddle*

"Let's go home, Debbie."

—Ethan Edwards, *The Searchers*

"That'll be the day."

—Ethan Edwards, *The Searchers*

"I won't be wronged, I won't be insulted, and I won't be laid a hand on. I don't do these things to other people and I require the same from them."

—John Bernard Books, *The Shootist*

Confronting four outlaws, Rooster Cogburn is taunted with the words, "Bold talk for a one-eyed fat man"—Rooster responds, "Fill your hand you sonuvabitch!" and charges them with his reins in his teeth.

—Rooster Cogburn, *True Grit*

While holding a gun on a black man, Cahill says, "I ain't got a bigoted bone in my body; I'll blast you to hell as quick as any white man."

—J. D. Cahill, *Cahill, U.S. Marshall*

"I used to be a good cowhand, but things happen."

—Ringo Kid, *Stagecoach*

"Mon-sewer, you may not live long enough to hang."

—Ranger Capt. Jake Cutter, *The Comancheros*

"Forget it! He's just spittin' up words to see where they splatter."

—Ranger Capt. Jake Cutter, *The Comancheros*

"Yer beautiful in yer wrath! I shall keep you, and in responding to my passion, yer hatred will kindle into love."

—Genghis Kahn, *The Conqueror*

"You can't give the enemy a break. Send him to hell."
—Lt. Col. Benjamin Vandervoort,
The Longest Day

"I know I'm gonna use good judgment. I haven't lost my temper in forty years, but pilgrim you caused a lot of trouble this morning, might have got somebody killed . . . and somebody otta belt you in the mouth. But I won't, I won't . . . the hell I won't!" (He belts him in the mouth.)

—George Washington McLintock,
McLintock!

"Half the people in the world are women. Why does it have to be you that stirs me?"

—George Washington McLintock,
McLintock!

"And now, God help them, 'cause that's all the help they'll get from us."

—Gen. Mike Randolph, *Cast a Giant Shadow*

"I've never met one [a woman] yet that was half as reliable as a horse."

—Sam McCord, *North to Alaska*

"There'll be no locked doors between us, Mary Kate Thornton."

—Sean Thornton, *The Quiet Man*

"It ain't our ox that's getting gored" elicited this response: "Talk about whose ox is gettin' gored. Figure this. A fellow gets in the habit of gorin' oxes, it whets his appetite. He may come up north and gore yours."

—Col. Davy Crockett, *The Alamo*

"She reminds me of me!"

—Rooster Cogburn, *True Grit*

"Well, my tail feathers may droop a little and my waddle show, but I can still out crow anything in the barnyard."

—Rooster Cogburn, *Rooster Cogburn*

Anecdotes

*He's an American institution and nothing can topple
him. He has tremendous guts, he always has. There's the
Rock of Gilbraltar, the Empire State Building, and
Duke Wayne.*
—Andrew McLaglen

*I never saw Duke display hatred toward those who
scorned him. Oh, he could use some pretty salty
language, but he would not tolerate pettiness and hate.*
—President Ronald Reagan

*His image had as much impact in the world as many of
our presidents have had, but Duke was a great actor,
a great humanitarian, but always himself.
To be a friend was a lifetime thing.*
—Elizabeth Taylor

*I liked Wayne's wholeness, his style. As for his politics,
well—I suppose even cavemen felt a little admiration
for the dinosaurs that were trying to gobble them up.*
—Abbie Hoffman

FOLLOWING ARE a few of the anecdotes that abound about the Duke:

"I saw his loyalty in action many times. I remember that when Duke and Jimmy Stewart were on their way to my second inauguration as governor of California, they encountered a crowd of demonstrators under the banner of the Vietcong flag. Jimmy had just lost a son in Vietnam. Duke excused himself for a moment and walked into the crowd. In a moment there was no Vietcong flag."

—President Ronald Reagan

"They have beautiful sunsets in Durango, and I was making a movie with my father. There was this big wooden rocking chair on the porch where my father stayed, and he said to me, 'Come up here, sit down, and look at this sunset.' And I told him that I couldn't. There was work to do for the next day's shoot, and it was my job to make sure everything was in place. He said, 'Let me tell you—the work will be there. It's going to be there tomorrow, but this sunset isn't going to be there. Don't miss it.' He had balance in his life. He was in sync with the world around him."

—Michael Wayne

Ward Bond, Wayne's lifelong friend, and the Duke enjoyed playing practical jokes on each other. One time Bond made a bet with Wayne that they could stand on opposite sides of a newspaper and Wayne wouldn't be able to hit him. After Wayne accepted the challenge, Bond placed the newspaper in a doorway and placed Wayne on one end. He then walked through the doorway, turned, and slammed the door in Wayne's face. Shouting from the other side, he yelled, "Try and hit me now!" Wayne's response was immediate: his fist came through the door, knocking Bond to the floor and winning the bet by a knockdown.

Following his debate with President Jimmy Carter, Republican candidate Ronald Reagan was asked by a reporter what it felt like being on the same stage with the president. Reagan smiled and said, "It was nothing; after all, I've been on stage with John Wayne."

The Duke loved the poetry of Walt Whitman, and one of his favorite passages was, "I contradict myself? Very well. . . . I can contradict myself. I am large; I contain multitudes."

Fellow actor Lee Marvin relates that working with Wayne on a movie was a great pleasure because they had a lot in common. Not only did they share great drinking bouts, but also they had "culture" in common. They both enjoyed reading and appreciated works of art and had a shared interest in history. Marvin said that Wayne had told him that he also enjoyed biographies and had read everything ever written by Winston Churchill. When Marvin told Wayne, "You're not the illiterate, uneducated ignoramus you'd like people to think," Duke replied, "Neither are you, let's keep it to ourselves or we'll ruin our image."

Bud Boetticher, a visitor to the set of *Rio Bravo*, tells of the effect of Wayne's powerful presence and how it could negatively affect his fellow actors. In a scene taking place in a saloon, Claude Aiken says to Wayne, "So what are you gonna do now?" Wayne came back without missing a beat and said, "Well the first thing I'm gonna do is change the tone of my voice. If all you (expletives) are going to talk just like me." It was amazing how the other actors started talking like Duke without even realizing it.

Playing a Roman soldier in *The Greatest Story Ever Told*, Wayne was to look up at the cross and say, "Truly, this man was the son of God." The director George Stevens wasn't happy with Wayne's first take and told him to "put a little more awe into the line." When the cameras rolled again, Wayne grinned and looked up at the cross and drawled in a most un-Roman western accent, "Aaah, truly, this man was the son of God," sending everyone into hysterical laughter. His third take was perfect.

In response to questions about his nickname, Wayne said, "There have been a lot of stories about how I got to be called Duke. One was that I played the part of a duke in a school play—which I never did. Sometimes, they even said I was descended from royalty! It was a lot of rubbish. Hell, the truth is that I was named after a dog." Just like Indiana Jones it seems—Wayne and his dog, an Airedale terrier named Duke, walked to school together, and Wayne used to leave his dog at the nearby fire station while he was in class. The firemen took to calling them big Duke and little Duke. Since Wayne didn't like his first name of Marion anyway, he encouraged people to call him Duke. Wayne also said of the firefighters, "They were great guys. They used to give me milk—they'd say, 'take it home for your cat,' even though they knew I didn't have a cat."

Trying to get some sleep in a Las Vegas hotel before an early morning shoot, Wayne was kept awake by a loud party going on in the suite below him that was occupied by Frank Sinatra and friends. Each time he made a polite complaining phone call, the noise would abate for a while and then escalate. Finally, Wayne went downstairs and told Sinatra to stop the noise. A Sinatra bodyguard of Wayne's size moved aggressively toward him and said, "Nobody talks to Mr. Sinatra that way." Wayne looked at the man, turned as though to go, then turned back swiftly and backhanded the bodyguard, who dropped to the floor—the party noise stopped.

In 1972, the daughter of his friend Henry Fonda went to Hanoi and became known as "Hanoi Jane." When he saw the newspaper reports, all Wayne could think of was her father and how he must feel and saw that she would become infamous for her stand. However, not one to hold a grudge against those who disagreed with him, in 1978 when the Hollywood Women's Press Club asked him to present Jane Fonda with their

Golden Apple Award as female star of the year, he agreed to do it. When presenting her with the trophy, he said, "I have known her father for forty years, and therefore I had a special reason to watch her grow from childhood. Evidently I didn't make too much of an impression on her, and I'm certainly surprised to find her standing to the right side of me!"

Harry Carey Jr. tells of working with his mother, Olive Carey, and Wayne in *The Searchers* directed by John Ford; his father, Harry Carey, was an early idol and role model of Wayne's. At the end of the movie as he turns to go out the door, Wayne raised his left hand, reached across his chest, and grabbed his right arm at the elbow. "My dad did that a lot in movies when Wayne was just a kid in Glendale. It was just one take as natural as anything even though Ford wasn't expecting it, and my mom, looking on in the scene, never forgot this tribute to my dad."

Duke starred with Rock Hudson for the first time in *The Undefeated*, and Hudson was wary about working with Wayne, fearing homophobia. When they first met on the set, Wayne was standing in front of a small mirror putting on some natural lipstick. He turned to

Hudson, narrowed his eyes, and drawled, "Well, I hear you're a good bridge player." They developed a friendly relationship and became great friends. Later he was asked what he thought about Hudson's homosexuality, and he replied, "What Rock Hudson does—in the privacy of his own room—is his own business. He's a professional on the set and a real gentleman—and he plays a hell of a hand of bridge."

At times the Duke had a love-hate relationship with director John Ford. After filming *Red River* with Howard Hawks, Ford feigned surprise that Wayne could act and presented him with a birthday cake that year with one candle to mark his first year of mature acting. Wayne commented that he knew he had finally arrived.

Geraldine Page worked with Wayne in *Hondo* and became enchanted with him. She tells of a time when a storm came up on the Camargo set where they were shooting in a dry lake bed. The director immediately removed the American cast and crew and left the Mexican crew behind to take care of the equipment. Back at the motel, Wayne began to worry about the Mexicans being flooded, spending the night outside in the wet and cold. So, he woke up the caterer, and they made up some sandwiches and hot coffee and gathered several bottles of tequila; he then spent the night with the Mexicans, eating, singing, drinking, and telling stories—it was something out of a Wayne movie.

Lee Van Cleef tells of a memory he has of working with Wayne on *The Man Who Shot Liberty Valance*. They had a scene together where Van Cleef had to draw on him and Wayne would knock the gun out of his hand. Before the scene, Van Cleef told him, "I can draw this gun so fast you won't be able to clap your hands before I put it between them." Wayne replied, "I'd like to see you try that." With Lee Marvin counting, Van Cleef drew his gun and had it between Wayne's hands before he could clap them together, and Wayne said, "That's pretty damn good but since you're so fast, the scene won't work." Van Cleef then said, "It's ok, Duke. I'll slow down for you." Wayne laughed and replied, "That's right nice of you to help an old actor out."

Early on, John Ford had hired Wayne as a prop man before letting him play an extra and stuntman in his films. In 1929, both displayed support for Stepin Fetchit, an African American actor who had a role in the film. Unusual for the times, Ford arranged to have him housed on location at Annapolis with the rest of the crew in a residence for distinguished visitors, and Wayne filled in and acted as his "dresser." No grumbling was allowed or heard on the set. Throughout both their careers, they continued to be unbiased regarding race and even set aside their own political differences when working together.

A legend himself, Denver Pyle had a role in *The Alamo* as one of the men from Tennessee. He revered John Wayne, and he was almost starstruck as he worked with him. When Wayne heard about it, he was amazed: "I'm in awe of Mr. Pyle! Besides, he's bigger than me!"

One night on the *North to Alaska* set, after eating a steak and drinking a bottle of wine, Wayne joined a poker game with the crew, drinking and laughing until well into the early morning hours. However, at 8:00 a.m., the fifty-three-year-old actor was on the set, makeup completed, and in costume. Filming was delayed, however, as the crew struggled in, and the Duke proudly declared, "Well, here come the kids. I had to tuck them in last night." And then he said under his breath, "The country's going soft!"

As a sixteen-year-old, Natalie Wood played the part of Debbie in *The Searchers*, and she tells how Wayne, who played Ethan Edwards, was a giant to her and how, near the end, he picked her up as if she was a doll. She was pretty frightened because he had this look of hatred, and she was thinking how easily he could crush her. Then, as he saw his former love in her eyes, an almost indefinable gentleness came over him as he cradled her and said, "Debbie, let's go home." Natalie said of Wayne that she had heard that he always played the same part but insisted from her own experience that "Mr. Wayne was a very fine actor."

During an appearance on television, the great dancer Gene Kelly was asked by the interviewer to name a man he thought of as being graceful. Perhaps the interviewer was expecting him to name a fellow dancer such as Fred Astaire or a ballet performer. Instead, Kelly replied, "John Wayne." He explained that the Duke moved with the grace of an athlete and the poise of a man who knew his strength and was confident enough to show himself as also tender and gentle.

Pilar Wayne tells of the time when the Duke once played an all-night poker game with the handler who owned the first Lassie and several others—Wayne won all the Lassies. The next morning, seeing the devastated man who had lost his livelihood, Wayne gave them all back after a good laugh.

Wayne spent his 1974 Thanksgiving with his ranching partner, Louis Johnson, who had a party for him and their cattlemen friends. That afternoon, with a drink in his hand, Wayne lost his footing at the edge of the indoor swimming pool and fell in. Immediately some-one yelled, "Sheee-it. He can't walk on water after all!" Duke bellowed with laughter louder than anyone else—he loved being treated as any other cowhand.

Two days after winning an Oscar for his portrayal of Rooster Cogburn, Wayne returned to the set of the film he was acting in at the time, *Rio Lobo*. A car picked him up, and as they drove up to the location, he saw that the entire cast and crew were assembled in front of the adobe church—everyone, including the horse, wore an eye patch. The crowd was clapping and whistling congratulations. A shocked Wayne laughed heartily at first and then became teary eyed at the gesture.

The Duke went quail shooting one evening with some friends, including Ward Bond, whom he had known since his college days. Bond was dressed in cowboy boots, and he was having a difficult time walking and was lagging behind. The little hunting group went on to a secluded spot where they wouldn't bother anyone. Suddenly, Duke thought he saw a cottontail, so he fired and a huge roar was heard. Ward Bond turned out to be the cottontail, and his backside had been splattered with buckshot. Duke thought he had mortally wounded him by the noise and jumping around that Bond displayed. In a great panic, Bond was taken to a doctor in a nearby town. For some reason, the ether wasn't knocking out the excited Bond, so his friends got some whiskey, force-fed him, and held him down while the doctor removed the buckshot. He made a quick recovery. The moral of the story is that even an American icon can make a mistake—just as well as a vice president.